The
One
Day

POETRY BY DONALD HALL

THE ONE DAY
A Poem in Three Parts

Donald Hall

TICKNOR & FIELDS   NEW YORK   1988

For information about permission to reproduce selections
from this book, write to Permissions, Ticknor & Fields,
52 Vanderbilt Avenue, New York, New York 10017.

LIBRARY OF CONGRESS CATALOGING-IN-PUBLICATION DATA

Hall, Donald, date.
  The one day : a poem in three parts / Donald Hall.
    p. cm.
  ISBN 0–89919–817–1. ISBN 0–89919–816–3 (pbk.)
  I. Title.
PS3515.A3152054 1988
811'.54 — dc19   88–10130
                CIP

PRINTED IN THE UNITED STATES OF AMERICA

P 10 9 8 7 6 5 4 3 2 1

Portions of this poem have previously appeared elsewhere. An earlier version
of "Shrubs Burnt Away" first appeared in *Kenyon Review* and also was
published in *The Happy Man*, copyright © 1986 by Donald Hall, reprinted by
permission of Random House, Inc. From "Four Classic Texts": "Prophecy"
first appeared in *The Paris Review*; "Pastoral" in *The Southern California
Anthology*; "History" in *The New Yorker*; and "Eclogue" in *The Gettysburg
Review*. "To Build a House" first appeared in *The Iowa Review*.

To Jane Kenyon

Each man bears the entire form of man's estate.

— Michel de Montaigne

Every human being is a colony.

— Pablo Picasso

When the coach clattered into the inn-yard, the old gentleman hastened to finish his story: "It remained silent thereafter." Gathering his luggage he prepared to depart . . . adding, "There are other voices, within my own skull I daresay. A woman speaks clearly from time to time; I do not know her name. Especially there speaks a man who resembles me overmuch yet is distinctly not me." So saying he departed . . .

— Abbé Michel de Bourdeille

I

Shrubs
Burnt
Away

What then are the situations, from the representation of which, though accurate, no poetical enjoyment can be derived? They are those in which the suffering finds no vent in action; in which a continuous state of mental distress is prolonged, unrelieved by incident, hope, or resistance; in which there is everything to be endured, nothing to be done.

— Matthew Arnold

Mi-t'o Temple after thirty li. A most desolate spot . . . For fear of them hiding tigers, all trees and shrubs have been burnt.

— Hsu Hsia-k'o

"Once a little boy and his sister" — my mother lay
on top of the quilt, narrow and tense, whispering —
"found boards piled up, deep in the woods, and nails,
and built a house for themselves, and nobody knew
how they built their house each day in the woods . . ."
I listened and fell asleep, like a baby full of milk,
and carried the house into sleep where I built it
board by board all night, each night
from the beginning; from a pile of boards I built it,
painted it, put doorknobs on it . . .

As I sit by myself, middle-aged in my yellow chair,
staring at the vacant book of the ceiling, unfit
to work or love, aureoled with cigarette smoke
in the unstoried room, I daydream to build
the house of dying: The old man alone in the farmhouse
makes coffee, whittles, walks, and cuts an onion
to eat between slices of bread. But the white loaf
on the kitchen table comes undone: —
Milk leaks; flour and yeast draw apart;
sugar and water puddle the table's top.

Bullied, found wanting, my father drove home
from his work at the lumberyard weeping,
and shook his fist over my cradle: "He'll do
what he wants to do!" — and kept to it twenty
years later, still home from his job hopeless
in outrage, smoking Luckies, unable to sleep
for coughing. Forty years I have waked
to the shallow light, forty years of the day's
aging; today I observe for the first time
white hair that grows from my wrist's knuckle.

I lay in my dark bedroom hearing trees scrape
like Hauptmann's ladder on the gray clapboard.
Downstairs the radio diminished, Bing Crosby,
and I heard voices like logs burning, flames
rising and falling, one high and steady, one
urgent and quick. If I cried, if I called . . . I called
softly, sore in the wrapped dark, but there was **nothing**,
I was nothing, the light's line at the closed door faint.
I called again; I heard her steps: —
Light swept in like a broom from the opening door

and my head lay warm on her shoulder, and her breath
sang in my ear: — "A Long Long Trail A-winding";
"Backward Turn Backward O Time in Thy Flight . . ."
In the next room a drawer banged shut. When my father
lay dying at fifty-one, he could not deliver
the graduation speech at Adams Avenue School
near the house he was born in. As I took my father's
place, my head shook like a plucked wire.
I told the fourteen-year-olds:
"Never do anything except what you want to do."

I could not keep from staring out the window.
Teachers told my mother I was an intelligent girl,
if I would only apply myself. But I continued
to gaze at hills pushing upward, or to draw with my crayons.
In the third grade Mr. Blake came on Wednesdays;
he said I was the best young artist in the township.
At home when my mother made Parker House rolls
she let me mold scraps of dough on the oilcloth
of the kitchen table, and I shaped my first soft
rising edible sculptures: So my life started.

The year after my father burned in the wrecked car,
my mother came home early from the job she hated,
teaching bookkeeping at the secretarial college.
Sometimes she wept because she had flunked someone
she caught cheating. Each day I comforted her;
I was fifteen years old. I cooked supper for her —
hamburgers and hot dogs, baked beans, corn niblets.
Once I took a recipe from "Confidential Chat,"
using Ritz crackers, asparagus soup, and waterchestnuts.
She said I would make some man happy.

That was the year I stopped drawing. Sometimes at night
when she fell asleep I would look at my old portfolio
and cry, and pick up a pencil, and set it down.
Every night before supper we played Chinese checkers
and I beat her; she trembled lifting the marbles, only forty
years old. She came home exhausted, not wanting to play.
After a while we played no more checkers
and she collapsed early listening to her radio mysteries
in the blue leather lounger, with the vodka that ruptured
her liver through her abdomen ten years later.

Closing my eyes I recognize other citizens
and colonists: One is an actor, homosexual, in a rent-
controlled apartment near Sullivan Square; he waits
for the telephone — two weeks in General Hospital
as a kindly thoracic surgeon. In Woodbridge outside
New Haven another lives — ironic, uxorious, the five
children grown and gone; he waters his lawn with irony;
he works forty hours of irony a week and lives
to retire. Another died dropping from a parking structure
last April, climbing the parapet drunk with purpose.

When I was twelve I spent the summer on the farm,
painting watercolors all morning, all afternoon hoeing
the garden with my grandmother who told stories.
We fed the hens; we gathered eggs. Once we discovered
four hen-husks drained dry by a weasel.
That summer I painted One Hundred Views
of house, hill, and covered bridge. When my grandmother
woke me at six o'clock with black coffee
the day lay before me like a green alley of grass
through a meadow I invented by setting my foot to it.

When my mother came home from the drying-out hospital,
still convulsive, she took pills and talked without stopping.
She told me about her first breakdown
when she was nine years old. She had a nightmare
over and over again: Bearded men — who looked like the tramps
asking for bread and butter at the porch door
or like the gypsies camping in their wagons every summer —
made a circle around her, and the circle grew smaller
as the bearded men shuffled close. Every night
she woke up screaming, unable to stop. She knew

they wanted to cut her up for a patchwork quilt. Her mother
and father set a small cot beside their bed; when she woke
screaming they comforted her. The circle of men
came closer; even when she was awake in her mother's arms
the circle tightened; she heard her grandfather
tell somebody on the porch, "We're going to lose
our little girl." When she stopped crying her mother
pumped a cup of water. She remembered once
her mother brought water in an unwashed coffee cup
and there was sugar stuck in the bottom of the cup.

The Bee Gee, huge engine and tiny stub wings,
snapped around pylons in the Nationals; each year
they clipped more wing off. *On the Fourth of July,*
I turned nine years old. I was playing in the woods
with Bingo and Harold Johnson; Bingo had a crush on me.
We were chasing each other and ran into a clearing
and found Bingo and Harold's father and my mother
drunk, rolling in the grass with their clothes off.
Douglas Corrigan took off from Long Island, flight plan
filed for California, plane heavy with gasoline,

and flew to Ireland — Wrong-Way Corrigan:
a mistake, he claimed; no sense of direction . . .
Later we returned to the house with the grown-ups
and my father threw his old fashioned in my mother's face.
When I tried to run outside my uncle caught me
and set me on his lap; I kept on watching in my blue
shirt over my lace birthday blouse. For three years
a Pomona fireman worked weekends in his garage building
an airplane that used the motors from six lawnmowers.
The CAB refused a license; a strut washed up on Catalina.

My father ran from the house carrying a winebottle.
When he backed out of the driveway
he knocked the mailbox over. My mother got my uncle
to chase him along dirt roads at midnight
very fast; — I sat in the back seat, frightened.
He lost us but we knew where he was going. Wiley Post
and Will Rogers flew from the Walaka Lagoon; Innuit
found their bodies. In the Pacific, Navy patrol-planes
searched for Amelia Earhart while her Lockheed foundered
through fathoms with its cargo of helmeted corpses.

Now an old man walks on blacktop, farmhouse
to postoffice, by a ditch gray with late August grass.
Now he is a boy carrying his scythe to join
his grandfather mowing on the machine in the hayfield,
where he will trim around rocks. He tilts his blade
toward German prisoners, sleeping by day in ditches,
who escaped last week from the Canadian prison camp.
When he returns, old man again, to the farmhouse
by the strong cowbarn, past Aunt Bertha's cottage,
blond prisoners drink schnapps in the livingroom.

Now I told my wife: Consider me a wind that lifts
the square white houses up and spins them
into each other; or as a flood loosening houses
from their cellarholes; or as a fire that burns
white wooden houses down. I was content in the dark
livingroom, fixed in the chair with whiskey.
I claimed that the wind was out of control
while I looked through a window where the June trees
blew in the streetlight at two o'clock; leaves broke
from their stems but the trunk did not split open.

Now I declared that everywhere at two in the morning
men sat awake in yellow chairs, doing nothing,
while their wives lay upstairs in bed with open eyes.
Last night at the reception I glimpsed the made-up faces
of women I knew elsewhere — pale, shaking,
passionate, weeping. We understood together:
The world is a bed. In discontented peace,
in boredom and tolerance, only adultery proves
devotion by risk; only the pulse of betrayal
makes blood pelt in the chest as if with joy.

(Who is it that sets these words on blue-lined paper?
It is the old man in the room of bumpy wallpaper.
It is the girl who sits on her drunken mother's lap
or carries her grandmother's eggs. It is the boy who reads
the complete works of Edgar Allan Poe. It is the middle-
aged man motionless in a yellow chair, unable to read,
daydreaming the house of dying: The colony takes comfort
in building this house which does not exist, because
it does not exist — as I stare at the wrist's knuckle,
idle, without purpose, fixed in a yellow chair.)

At the exact millisecond when two cells fused
and multiplied, I started this house. Through years of milk
and potty I constructed foundations; *in Mr. Blake's
classroom I built it*; in vacant lots hopeless at football,
at Walter's Creek hunting for frogs and turtles,
under leaf's breath, in rotted leaves I built it;
in months at the worktable assembling model airplanes,
at the blackboard doing sums, *in blue summer painting
watercolors at my grandmother's I built this house.*
I build it over again, stiff in the permanent chair.

There was the dream of the party: a French farce,
frolic behind curtains, exits and entrances —
like a child fooling parents. I departed
alone on a bus that bumped down the white staircase
of the mansion over the bodies of three women
who stood complacent and pretty in the bus's way,
their faces familiar as photographs. When I looked
back from the bus's rear window at their bodies,
they waved to me although they were dead: —
They forgave me because no one was driving the bus.

My daughter curled in my lap, wailing and red,
six years old. My fifteen-year-old son's long legs
writhed from a chair as tears fell on his spectacles.
Their mother was leaving them . . . I
was leaving them. Their muscles contracted
knees to chin, as I watched from my distance,
and their limbs twitched and jerked in the velvet room.
My daughter wanted to see the place I had rented
to move to. She whirled among cheap furniture,
over bare linoleum, saying, "Cozy, cozy . . ."

It rains on Sunset Boulevard. I walk with the collar
of my jacket turned up. Topless go-go dancers twist
at the back of a bar, while men on the wet sidewalk
peer into the doorway at the young women's bodies,
their smooth skin intolerably altered by ointments
and by revolving orange and purple lights.
Lights bruise their thighs: — for three thousand years
these lights and ointments . . . I rejected
the comforts I had contrived for myself; I exchanged them
for a rain of small faces on the abandoned street.

I am a dog among dogs, and I whine about waking
to the six o'clock sun of summer, or brag
about Sinbad's adventures, for which I left houses
excessive with shrubbery, carpets, and mirrors.
Justifying myself I claim: After the breathless blue
of my father's face, I chose the incendiary flower:
Yellow flame budded from clapboard; therefore,
rain on the Boulevard. Now in the gray
continuous morning, water drips from the cindery houses
that wanted to bloom in the night. I stay up all night

at the Hollywood–La Brea Motel looking at television,
black-and-white war movies, Marines at Iwo,
sailors and blondes, B-24s; I do not understand
what happens. I listen to shills in blazers
with sixpenny London accents pitch acrylic while I drink
Scotch from the bottle. Studying a bikini'd
photograph on a matchbox, I dial BONNIE FASHION
MODEL AVAILABLE at four in the morning
from my vinyl room, and the answering service tells me
that Bonnie is out to lunch . . .

I take out my sketchbook as I wait for the plane
in a blockhouse at the airport's edge; then the cement
walls vibrate as if an earthquake shook them.
I understand: The plane from Chicago has crashed
trying to land. Immediately I watch a conveyor belt
remove bodies covered with brown army blankets
from the broken snake of the fuselage. One of the dead
sits up abruptly, points a finger at me,
and stares accusingly. It is an old man with an erection:
Then I notice that all of the dead are men.

Another self sits all day in a watchpocket
of cigarette smoke, staring at the wrist-knuckle,
in repetitious vacancy examining the ceiling, its cracks
and yellowed paint, unprinted emptiness rolling
as continuous as the ocean, no ship or landfall anywhere,
no bird or airplane. I climb from the yellow chair
to the bare bedroom and lie on my back smoking
and staring . . . until ice in a glass, golden whiskey,
euphoria, falling down, and sleep with two yellowjacketed
Nembutals pave the undreaming gilt road to nothing.

Therefore I envy an old man hedging and ditching
three hundred years ago in Devon. I envy the hedge
and the ditch. When my father came home
from the lumberyard, head shaking, fingers
yellow with Luckies, I begged him to play catch
with me. He smacked the pocket
of a catcher's mitt: "Put her there!" — and I threw
a fastball ten feet over his head. As he trotted
after the ball I waited, ashamed of being
wild: — enraged, apologetic, unforgiving.

When I was in my thirties, in love with the fires
that burned white houses down, desires and treacheries
passed the time. My children receded, waving. Janis
Joplin said, "It's always the same fucking day."
I counted divorces; I slept drugged sleep through years
of continual winter, frost in July and August, as in 1816,
the Poverty Year my grandmother's grandmother told of: —
The cornfield, frozen and planted again, froze yet again,
tomatoes pustulent on vines of August, hard frost
twelve months out of twelve, and "We ate the seedcorn."

During the gelid midsummers of middle-life, I saw
dream hayfields scattered with boxes long and narrow
like haybales; I stumbled in a darkness of waking dream
against these oblongs; under the full moon I gazed
at their luminous shapes, rounded on top with snow
like enormous loaves. Sitting in my chair I walked
in the corpsefield: babies among them,
old women, young men, mothers and fathers, corpses
of men and women. My stub-winged airplanes crashed.
When I slept without drugs, cannibal dreams awoke me.

Now in my mind a solitary old man walks back and forth
from linoleum to carpet to linoleum again.
In Laurel Canyon I stand smiling, shifting my weight,
among middle-aged rich who eat shrimp curled on ice,
who wear tartan jackets or earrings coded to their shoes.
They do not notice how I descend to the rootcellar
with its dirt floor where a mirror hangs in the gloom;
I make out a white beard and glasses that reflect
nothing. But when I touch my chin my face is smooth;
I rejoin the party; I smile; I am careful drinking.

Nothing remains except a doll strangled on fencewire.
Night after night I sleep on pills and wake exhausted:
Rage weighs its iron on my chest. I cannot enter
the orchard's farmhouse on the hill, or find the road
vanished under burdock. I burn another house
and self-pity exhausts me. Bonnie orders a burger.
I pour the first tumbler over icecubes that dull the taste:
Roots of my hair go numb; numbness spreads downward
over the forehead's wrinkles past bloody eyes
to stomach, to wrist's white hair, to dead penis.

The world is a bed, I announced; my love agreed.
A hundred or a thousand times our eyes encountered:
Each time the clothes sloughed off, anatomies
of slippery flesh connected again on the world's bed
and the crescent of nerves described itself
in the ordinary curve of bliss. We were never alone;
we were always alone. If we were each the same
on the world's bed, if we were each manikins of the other,
then the multitude was one and one was the multitude;
many and one we performed procedures of comfort.

I am very happy. I dance supine on my bed laughing
until four in the morning, when the bottle is empty
and the liquor store closed on Hollywood and La Brea.
I must not drive the car for cigarettes; —
therefore I lurch a mile to the All-Nite Laundro-Mart
and falter back coughing. In the morning I lie
waking dozing twisted in the damp workclothes
of lethargy, loathing, and the desire to die.
My father's head shook like a plucked wire:
"Never do anything except what you want to do."

I am sad in the convenient white kitchen, dreaming
that I weep as I start making dinner, setting things out.
The children themselves weep, bringing their sentences
on small folded squares of paper.
They will take pills to die without disturbance.
I help them count the pills out, and arrange
pillows for their comfort as they become sleepy.
While I slice onions and peppers on the breadboard,
someone whose identity hovers just out of sight, the way
a beekeeper's mask darkens a face,

walks up the busy street and enters the kitchen
to instruct me in preparing the children.
The visitor picks up the long rag doll and with scissors
carefully cuts the doll's limbs at the joints,
teaching me expertly, with anatomical explanations
and a scientific vocabulary, while measuring and cutting
the model, then places the doll's parts
on a high shelf, arranged with the gaps of dismemberment
visible, so that I may consult it while cutting,
as I must do, as it appears that I want to do.

II

Four
Classic
Texts

Of the opposites that which tends to birth or creation is called war or strife. That which tends to destruction by fire is called concord or peace.

— Heraclitus

Poetry is preparation for death.

— Nadezhda Mandelstam

PROPHECY

I will strike down wooden houses; I will burn aluminum
clapboard skin; I will strike down garages
where crimson Toyotas sleep side by side; I will explode
palaces of gold, silver, and alabaster: — the summer
great house and its folly together. Where shopping malls
spread plywood and plaster out, and roadhouses
serve steak and potatoskins beside Alaska king crab;
where triangular flags proclaim tribes of identical campers;
where airplanes nose to tail exhale kerosene,
weeds and ashes will drowse in continual twilight.

I reject the old house and the new car; I reject
Tory and Whig together; I reject the argument
that modesty of ambition is sensible because the bigger
they are the harder they fall; I reject Waterford;
I reject the five and dime; I reject Romulus and Remus;
I reject Martha's Vineyard and the slamdunk contest;
I reject leaded panes; I reject the appointment made
at the tennis net or on the seventeenth green; I reject
the Professional Bowlers Tour; I reject matchboxes;
I reject purple bathrooms with purple soap in them.

I reject Japanese smoked oysters, potted chrysanthemums
allowed to die, Tupperware parties, Ronald McDonald,
Kaposi's sarcoma, the Taj Mahal, Holsteins wearing
electronic necklaces, the Algonquin, Tunisian aqueducts,
Phi Beta Kappa keys, the Hyatt Embarcadero, carpenters
jogging on the median, and betrayal that engorges
the corrupt heart longing for criminal surrender.
I reject shadows in the corner of the atrium
where Phyllis or Phoebe speaks with Billy or Marc
who says that afternoons are best although not reliable.

Your children will wander looting the shopping malls
for forty years, suffering for your idleness,
until the last dwarf body rots in a parking lot.
I will strike down lobbies and restaurants in motels
carpeted with shaggy petrochemicals
from Maine to Hilton Head, from the Skagit to Tucson.
I will strike down hang gliders, wiry adventurous boys;
their thigh bones will snap, their brains
slide from their skulls. I will strike down
families cooking wildboar in New Mexico backyards.

Then landscape will clutter with incapable machinery,
acres of vacant airplanes and schoolbuses, ploughs
with seedlings sprouting and turning brown through colters.
Unlettered dwarves will burrow for warmth and shelter
in the caves of dynamos and Plymouths, dying
of old age at seventeen. Tribes wandering
in the wilderness of their ignorant desolation,
who suffer from your idleness, will burn your illuminated
missals to warm their rickety bodies.
Terrorists assemble plutonium because you are idle

and industrious. The whip-poor-will shrivels
and the pickerel chokes under the government of self-love.
Vacancy burns air so that you strangle without oxygen
like rats in a biologist's bell jar. The living god sharpens
the scythe of my prophecy to strike down red poppies
and blue cornflowers. When priests and policemen
strike my body's match, Jehovah will flame out;
Jehovah will suck air from the vents of bombshelters.
Therefore let the Buick swell until it explodes;
therefore let anorexia starve and bulimia engorge.

When Elzira leaves the house wearing her tennis dress
and drives her black Porsche to meet Abraham,
quarrels, returns to husband and children, and sobs
asleep, drunk, unable to choose among them, —
lawns and carpets will turn into tar together
with lovers, husbands, and children.
Fat will boil in the sacs of children's clear skin.
I will strike down the nations, astronauts and judges;
I will strike down Babylon, I will strike acrobats,
I will strike algae and the white birches.

Because professors of law teach ethics in dumbshow,
let the colonel become president; because chief executive
officers and commissars collect down for pillows,
let the injustice of cities burn city and suburb;
let the countryside burn; let the pineforests of Maine
explode like a kitchenmatch and the Book of Kells turn
ash in a microsecond; let oxen and athletes
flash into grease: — I return to Appalachian rocks;
I shall eat bread; I shall prophesy through millennia
of Jehovah's day until the sky reddens over cities:

Then houses will burn, even houses of alabaster;
the sky will disappear like a scroll rolled up
and hidden in a cave from the industries of idleness.
Mountains will erupt and vanish, becoming deserts,
and the sea wash over the sea's lost islands
and the earth split open like a corpse's gassy
stomach and the sun turn as black as a widow's skirt
and the full moon grow red with blood swollen inside it
and stars fall from the sky like wind-blown apples, —
while Babylon's managers burn in the rage of the Lamb.

PASTORAL

Marc: Shepherd and shepherdess, I with my pipe and song,
you leaning on your crook, in the kitchen's
hot valley among slaveboys and electric knives,
now the young husband kisses the young wife
he is not married to. As our tissues swell with blood,
as lubricant juices collect, we admire
important words: But the chiefest of these is love.
We discover in twenty years of assignations and replicas —
O Phyllis, O Phoebe, O Elzira — adventure or danger
which we confuse with passion, gifts exchanged,

Phyllis: and exchanged again. As the blood pelts, we confer;
and we pull off our clothes like opening junk mail.
The world is a bed — O Abraham, O Marc, O Billy —
where the multitude repeats itself for shepherd
and shepherdess, you with your pipe, I leaning on my crook
in the meadow; you leading your herd in summer
from valley to mountain, in autumn to valley again;
I kneeling to drink from the pool, hiding my face.
Of course I never balanced food and clothing
on my head as I led my children into stone hills,

Marc: away from airplanes. Of course my manager clearcuts
the forest and paves the garden; your broker ploughs
hillsides and destroys millennial loam for a crop
of corn. Of course I couldn't kill a rat with my putter
even if the rat shuddered in my daughter's crib.
You never braided rope in your hut for the beaked ships.
I never walked twenty miles through snow to hear
my president speak from the train's observation platform.
Now your green stationwagon, steady as a battering ram,
enters the garage painted by college students,

Phyllis: and I carry, my dearest, the supermarket's paperbags
into my clean kitchen; I align the cans on shelves
just so. I set the oven for two hours and ten minutes
while I cross-country. Dryads with slim exact
hips and hair assemble in my livingroom for bridge.
I am cheerful in order to be approved of. We forget
every skill we acquired over ten thousand years of labor.
I practice smiling; I forget how to milk a goat.
You forget how to construct aqueduct, temple, and cloaca.
We vote for the candidate who vows to abolish caritas.

Marc: I live in an unfenced compound among swineherds
and milkmaids identical in age, income, and education.
I am unacquainted with anyone who lives in a trailer
or wears a tattoo, except for Joseph who mows
my grass, whom I fear and despise. O Phyllis, O Elzira,
you never sat by a cooling stove while the clock struck
to study the word by candlelight. I never doubted
that money excused anything done to acquire it.
I meet the church vestry or the faculty of engines
smiling and joshing, full of hate, resentment, and envy.

Phyllis: My Hermes, you sit with your pipes pocketed at committee
meetings and eat nonbiodegradable doughnuts and drink
whitened coffee without protest. You play sets of tennis
with the director you dislike, and laugh shaking your head
as your baseline shots continually fall past the baseline.
You make rules, piper, by which you cannot be fired.
I cheat my employer; I quit and take unemployment
because I deserve it. You exploit your employees.
My friend in the city attorney's office reduces the charges.
You weep, my love, chained to the trireme's oar.

Marc: I fly with my family to San Juan for a week attended
by Moriscos. Drunk after the party, I fumble to embrace
the babysitter, taking her home, who will not sit
for my children again. I choose a girl from Records
instead, who is twenty-three and thinks I am rich.
Later when I am bored I disengage myself,
sending her presents. Ingratiating to boss, insulting
to employees, I endure my days without pleasure
or purpose, finding distraction in Rodeo Drive, in
duplicate bridge, in gladiators, and in my pastoral song.

HISTORY

When the knife slipped and cut deeply into the fingerpad
as he whittled a stick or trimmed ham from the bone,
at first he felt nothing, aware only of the nearly insensible
line on the skin. Always he imagined for one heartbeat
that he might undo the error and prevent the upsurge
of consequent blood: Such was the character of Juvenis,
who remembered always the doomed legions marching
as they left the city, their big arms swinging, or daydreamed
that the airplane halted inches from the rockface,
like the photograph of an airplane. In my only vision,

I Senex await calmly the formation rising rounded
from the finger's tip: — brilliant, certain, bountiful.
Now, pacing my battlements among sentries, I observe
how terrorists burn athletes; terrorists dynamite
the former ambassador of the executed prime minister;
terrorists sentence the kidnapped president for crimes
against the children they will never father or mother:
They shoot him through the head and stuff his body
into a Japanese sedan's trunk on a suburban street
where the regime's corrupt engines sniff him out.

In the trench there were several corpses. This was in France.
The heels of one stuck out from the dirt of the trenchwall,
the scalp of another. The most dreadful thing we saw
was an arm in field-gray with a hand, dead-white and wearing
a signet ring, that protruded from the wall of a saphead.
Wherever we dug for our safety, we dug into corpses,
more ours than the French. Whenever a mine exploded,
a chowder of flesh splashed through fog and gunsmoke to mark
our positions. Shreds of a Frenchman hung from the branch
of an apple tree. This was in May. This was in Vauquois.

For four hundred years and sixteen generations, I kept
my castle while vassals baked flatbread.
Hoplites protected the confluence of rivers. When plague
squatted in the streets, or when the brawn of Germany
crossed the river to cut soldiers and horses,
peasants and pigs turned wild in the hills. Drought starved,
flood drowned: — Then shires rose in the valleys again.
Bowmen and arquebusiers left bones in the Low Countries.
Seven generations built the wall. For a hundred years
redheaded barbarians walked through a gap in the wall; —

but Danegeld accumulated for bribes and fortifications.
Cabbages kept over winter. Grapes ripened into wine.
Boys gathered the eggs of birds in the June twilights.
Oaks cut for the cathedral roof left acorns behind
for pigs in the diocesan forest; then oaks grew
three centuries under the care of foresters, father and son,
to replace cathedral beams when the deathwatch beetle
chewed them hollow. And now when my managers fly
to Chicago on Tuesday and divorce in Santo Domingo
on Wednesday and cremate their stepchildren on Thursday

without learning on Friday the names their grandmothers
were born to — they weep, they drink a Manhattan straight up,
they tremble strapped to electrodes on a table.
When he assumed the throne Juvenis concentrated
on cost-effective methods for exterminating barbarians
under the boy's illusion that he might establish
permanent boundaries. When his Reichsmarschall Hanno
concluded the Rhine, Juvenis required him to find
a defensible durable allweather overland traderoute
from Cornwall to Cathay: Tin boxes preserved

aromas of Lapsang Souchong. John Ball and Spartacus
assemble plutonium for love, constructing a device
to reverse history's river. Titus Manlius scourged
and beheaded his own son for disobedient heroism.
We carried Bhutto to the gallows on a stretcher.
He weighed eighty-seven pounds, a sufficient weight;
he asked the hangman to expedite the matter.
Our imperial goal is simple and simple our mottoes:
PEACE FOR ETERNITY   NOT LIBERTY BUT ORDER.
Meantime as president-emperor I Senex employ

in the execution of governance the expedients
of postponement and triage: — These are the rules of rule.
What in our youth we considered solutions, what our public
relations officers with flourishing trumpets call
"Triumphs of Diplomacy," or "Our Leader's Military Genius,"
are stavings-off. When we stopped supplies for our camp
besieged on the Blue Nile, we gained petroleum and wheat
for the Manchurian campaign; Masada proved no obstacle,
nor the Wall. We strangled Vercingetorix
to purchase half a year. If a thousand decapitations

lilies
nd peonies;
lders.
spread
nt
und
lf,
n pressure
liver
tassels,

emselves
pigs of autumn.
will restore
her husband,

circle
ration,
increase
nptying
nter, spring.

provide us a century of grain growing, water progressing
along aqueducts, and cattle freshening each spring,
who will not unbind the fasces and sharpen the axe?
Greek fire burnt Saracens at Byzantium's castle
and swamps over the same ages advanced and receded —
as now in the sour pond a pickerel chokes; as now
a whip-poor-will dies unhatched in her frail shell.
Whenever mobs rise against torturers and murderers,
torturers and murderers rise to take their places
and Blues massacre Greens. Men enslave women

again and chop the beggar's hands off and tie
the homosexual's wrists to a killing post
and execute him with prostitutes and moneylenders.
Our former prime minister is dispatched by a single jurist
who empties a machinegun into his stomach.
Our Leader sends a note to the Arbiter, his obedient
counsellor, who opens his wrist in the bath while speaking
wittily with his entourage. But he dies too fast:
Slaves bandage his wrists. Remembering purpose at dawn,
he removes the gauze. Tiberius beheads six Jew doctors.

By Palmer Canyon the lemons in the irrigated groves
grow smaller each year. Here is the Republic's grave,
boneyard of Erasmus and Hume, Florentine gold
and azure, Donatello's bodily marble, graves of money
and liberty. Vertical barbarians ascend, the child armie
of passive ignorance. I Senex, president-emperor,
peering through cataracts, note that Greek fire has onl
for the moment prevented Viking and Turk and Bolsh
who scale my fortifications with devoted outrage
and howling for plunder break the small-paned windo

poppies, green flames of asparagus, and
extravagant in breezes that waver corn
and Holsteins dribble from abundant
From the cradle daffodils and millet w
like water after blue rain in April, eff
withdraw from air, the stream underg
with its eight-sided molecules purify it
and a fountain of clearness rise by its
into single light. Garlic will swell and
garlic at the ninth month, Indian corn

swollen grapes turn purple and plump
into wine, and the oak's acorns fatten f
By seed, by swelling and damp, the ch
bride to bridegroom and oldwife embr
familiar skin rub against skin, ecstatic
adventure repeat itself, telling the flesh
that coils into sleep, withdrawal and r
to gather desire again. Work and love
as grass enlarges in sun and downpour
itself to swell again: summer, autumn,

provide us a century of grain growing, water progressing
along aqueducts, and cattle freshening each spring,
who will not unbind the fasces and sharpen the axe?
Greek fire burnt Saracens at Byzantium's castle
and swamps over the same ages advanced and receded —
as now in the sour pond a pickerel chokes; as now
a whip-poor-will dies unhatched in her frail shell.
Whenever mobs rise against torturers and murderers,
torturers and murderers rise to take their places
and Blues massacre Greens. Men enslave women

again and chop the beggar's hands off and tie
the homosexual's wrists to a killing post
and execute him with prostitutes and moneylenders.
Our former prime minister is dispatched by a single jurist
who empties a machinegun into his stomach.
Our Leader sends a note to the Arbiter, his obedient
counsellor, who opens his wrist in the bath while speaking
wittily with his entourage. But he dies too fast:
Slaves bandage his wrists. Remembering purpose at dawn,
he removes the gauze. Tiberius beheads six Jew doctors.

By Palmer Canyon the lemons in the irrigated groves
grow smaller each year. Here is the Republic's grave,
boneyard of Erasmus and Hume, Florentine gold
and azure, Donatello's bodily marble, graves of money
and liberty. Vertical barbarians ascend, the child armies
of passive ignorance. I Senex, president-emperor,
peering through cataracts, note that Greek fire has only
for the moment prevented Viking and Turk and Bolshevik
who scale my fortifications with devoted outrage
and howling for plunder break the small-paned windows.

ECLOGUE

Muses of Sicily, inspiration of father Theocritus
who muttered and meditated in Alexandria's pastures: —
Help me proclaim the child. Not everyone prays for fire
or adores the styrofoam cup and its trash compactor.
Equally we understand that the pinecone has its enemies,
that oxen and Rhode Island Reds resist affection
because they die. If we praise trees let us praise
the acorns of generation. While the Sybil sings
the music of what happens, while Senex brags and grumbles
of millennia and legions, the jig of centuries

slows down, entropy's tune; and I sing before midnight,
before solstice, when the great year will regenerate
stone-heavy men and women from caves in oblivion's hills
to smelt iron again, to refine tools as fire discovers
the invented forge: iron, tin, bronze, silver.
New ages of metal will spiral with wars and prophets,
with heroes that poets sing of: — blind, scraping the bow
across the gusla. When the great year turns, the months
will lose their numbers, each hour outlast a season,
spring and summer upthrust from new earth ten million

poppies, green flames of asparagus, and lilies
extravagant in breezes that waver corn and peonies;
and Holsteins dribble from abundant udders.
From the cradle daffodils and millet will spread
like water after blue rain in April, effluent
withdraw from air, the stream underground
with its eight-sided molecules purify itself,
and a fountain of clearness rise by its own pressure
into single light. Garlic will swell and deliver
garlic at the ninth month, Indian corn fly tassels,

swollen grapes turn purple and plump themselves
into wine, and the oak's acorns fatten for pigs of autumn.
By seed, by swelling and damp, the child will restore
bride to bridegroom and oldwife embrace her husband,
familiar skin rub against skin, ecstatic
adventure repeat itself, telling the flesh's circle
that coils into sleep, withdrawal and restoration,
to gather desire again. Work and love will increase
as grass enlarges in sun and downpour, emptying
itself to swell again: summer, autumn, winter, spring.

III

To
Build
a
House

We consider that we have succeeded when hysterical misery turns into ordinary unhappiness.

— Sigmund Freud

A model! A model! What in hell would I do with a model? When I need to check something I go to my wife and lift her chemise.

— Aristide Maillol

Gazing at May's blossoms, imagining bounty of McIntosh,
I praise old lilacs rising in woods beside cellarholes;
I praise toads. I predict the telephone call
that reports the friend from childhood cold on a staircase.
I praise children, grandchildren, and just-baked bread.
I praise fried Spam and onions on slices of Wonder Bread;
I praise your skin. I predict the next twenty years,
days of mourning, long walks growing slow and painful.
I reject twenty years of mid-life; I reject rejections.
The one day stands unmoving in sun and shadow.

When I rise at eight o'clock my knuckles are stiff.
I sit for an hour wearing my nightgown in a sunny chair.
Hot water from the faucet, black coffee, and two aspirin
unstick my fingerjoints, and by these hands I join
the day that will never return. This is the single
day that extends itself, intent as an animal listening
for food, while I chisel at alabaster. All day I know
where the sun is. To seize the hour, I must cast myself
into work that I love, as the keeper hurls
horsemeat to the lion: — I am meat, lion, and keeper.

This afternoon the king and queen of Norway drove
downtown from their consulate to my studio. As we sat
drinking tea together, they were fastidious and democratic;
I had been told: It was not required to curtsy . . .
When the entourage disappeared into Third Avenue
I changed into jeans and climbed on my sore ankle
to the marble under the skylight. Matisse said, "Work
is paradise"; Rodin, "To work is to live without dying";
Flaubert, "It passes the time." For three hours
my mallet tapped while Donatello hovered above me.

There are ways to get rich: Find an old corporation,
self-insured, with capital reserves. Borrow
to buy: Then dehire managers; yellow-slip maintenance;
pay public relations to explain how winter is summer;
liquidate reserves and distribute cash in dividends:
Get out, sell stock for capital gains, reward the usurer,
and look for new plunder — leaving a milltown devastated,
workers idle on streetcorners, broken equipment, no cash
for repair or replacement, no inventory or credit.
Then vote for the candidate who abolishes foodstamps.

I embrace the creation, not for what it signifies,
but for volume and texture thrusting up
from the touched places. I marry the creation that stays
in place to be worked at, day after day.
The sparrow lights on my fire escape once and once only; —
there is only the one self; my day is to carve it.
That my mother disintegrated while I watched her
flies past my window once; that I burned white houses
in middle-life flies past my barred window once.
To know how the sparrow flies turns hours to marble.

After the Constitutional Convention in Philadelphia
the delegates started for home on horseback and in carriages,
for the former colonies of Massachusetts and Virginia,
for York State. They visited with friends telling stories.
They traveled all day; at nightfall they rested in taverns.
The moon waxed and waned; days grew long and shortened again;
it snowed; spring melted snow revealing gray grass.
Some sold horses to board steamboats working the rivers,
then disembarked for trains that shook out sparks
setting fire to grassy plain, sheepbarn, and farmhouse.

Some delegates hitched rides chatting with teamsters;
some flew stand-by and wandered stoned in O'Hare
or borrowed from King Alexander's National Bank: None
returned to plantation, farm, or townhouse.
They wandered weary until they encountered each other
again, converging on Hollywood Boulevard bordered with bars
in their absurd clothing like movie extras, Federalist
and Republican descending the cloverleaf together
to engage another Convention at the Hollywood–La Brea Motel —
wearing their nametags, befuddled, unable to argue.

There are ways to get by. When we bought this grownover
orchard from Bone's widow, we burnt birch the first winter
and worked odd-jobs part-time: sugaring, logging, substitute
teaching, schoolbus driving. The first summer we culled
old trees past saving (next winter we kept ourselves warm
in the scent of applewood); others we trimmed and topdressed.
Next spring we set out three hundred semidwarves
in the old hayfield that sloped north by the disused
railroad under the pasture turned into woodlot: McIntosh
mostly, New Hampshire's goodness, October's fiery compacted

appleflesh; Cortland, Empire, Strawberry, Astrakhan,
Baldwin, Spy . . . We order our days by the paradisal
routine of apples: from winter of pies and cider
through spring's trim and exaltation of blossom,
through summer's attention and repair: then picking
with neighbors, selling at roadside, packing for market . . .
We age among apples — in dread of icestorm, wet snow
in May, drought, August wind forcing an early drop; wary
of bark-eating deer, of bears that break branches climbing.
From the first orchard to the last is one day and eternity.

Smoke rises all day from two chimneys above us.
You stand by the stove looking south, through bare branches
of McIntosh, Spy, and Baldwin. You add oak logs
to the fire you built at six in the castiron stove.
At the opposite end of the same house, under another chimney,
I look toward the pond that flattens to the west
under the low sun of a January afternoon, from a notebook
busy with bushels and yields. All day in our opposite
rooms we carry wood to stoves, we pace up and down, we plan,
we set figures on paper — to converge at day's end

for kisses, bread, and talk; then we read in silence,
sitting in opposite chairs; then we turn drowsy.
Dreaming of tomorrow only, we sleep in the painted bed
while the night's frail twisting of woodsmoke assembles
overhead from the two chimneys, to mingle and disperse
as our cells will disperse and mingle when they lapse
into graveyard dirt. Meantime the day is double
in the work, love, and solitude of eyes
that gaze not at each other but at a third thing:
a child, a ciderpress, a book — work's paradise.

From north pole and south we approach each other;
Atlantic encounters Pacific, up meets down:
Where extremes meet we make our equator: — Your body
with narrow waist and carved shoulders, hips
comely, breasts outswooping; my body intent,
concentrated, and single. We enter this planisphere
without strangeness, betrayal, or risk; our bodies
after bright tumult float in shadow and repose
of watery sleep, skin's fury settling apart
and pole withdrawing to pole: A bed is the world.

Or: Buy fifty acres of pasture from the widower:
Survey, cut a road, subdivide; bulldoze the unpainted
barn, selling eighteenth-century beams with bark
still on them; bulldoze foundation granite that oxen sledded;
bulldoze stone walls set with lost skill; bulldoze the Cape
the widower lived in; bulldoze his father's seven-apple tree.
Drag the trailer from the scraggly orchard to the dump:
Let the poor move into the spareroom of their town
cousins; pave garden and cornfield; build weekend houses
for skiers and swimmers; build Slope 'n' Shore; name the new

road Blueberry Muffin Lane; build Hideaway Homes
for executives retired from pricefixing for General Electric
and migrated north out of Greenwich to play bridge
with neighbors migrated north out of Darien. Build huge
centrally heated Colonial ranches — brick, stone, and wood
confounded together — on pasture slopes that were white
with clover, to block public view of Blue Mountain.
Invest in the firm foreclosing Kansas that exchanges
topsoil for soybeans. Vote for a developer as United States
senator. Vote for statutes that outlaw visible poverty.

I crashed like my daredevil pilots; it was what
I wanted. For two years I moved among institutions,
admitted because of barbiturates — I took pills
to keep from dreaming — alcohol, and depression.
Electroshock blanked me out. If I worked my hands shook;
when I carved, my chisel slipped making errors: —
I contrived art out of errors. For five years I talked
with a white-haired woman three times a week.
Once toward the end I complained: "Is it possible, ever,
to be single-minded?" I spoke in discouragement, glimpsing

the erratum-slip on my psyche: "For love read hate
throughout; for hate read love." White eyebrows wavered:
"In this life?" she asked; but she added: "One day
you will love someone." I wept the whole hour with relief
and without confidence. If singleness is impossible, how
do we discover its idea that mocks us? Our longing
for being, beyond doubt and skepticism, assembles itself
from moments when the farmer scything alfalfa fills
with happiness as the underground cave fills with water;
or when we lose self in the hourless hour of love.

The one day clarifies and stays only when days depart:
"The days you work," said O'Keeffe, "are the best days."
Whole mornings disappeared through my hand into elmwood
before me. I did what I wanted: As my hand
strengthened I lost day after day that did not return
doubled and burnt in drug-time's cindery lapse.
No longer did I rage at my young father for dying
in the wrecked car. I slept all night without murder:
I talked with my friend; with my children I visited
the zoo on Wednesday; teasing I cooked them dinner.

When I was forty I married again. I kept him twelve years
until the occlusion snapped him off like a light. Now when
I am discontent, when the beekeeper's shadow approaches
up the desolate block, I number his disappearance
among the griefs and cinders where it belongs;
but neither the howl of loss nor ecstatic adventure remains
largest in store: My grainshed keeps the single
repeated green-valley day, repose of imaginable summer,
long hours not hours at all, vacant of number:
Like great Holsteins we chewed the voluptuous grass.

From burnt houses and blackened shrubs, green rises
like bread. Because the Revolution fails; because men
and women are corrupt and equal; because we eat topsoil
and Massachusetts smokes Virginia's tobacco; because
dancers twist in Alexandrine and millennial light
and lemons grow smaller in the groves; because the old
house burnt, because I burnt it, we carry green inside
from the hill: Potted plants on shelves braced
at every window or hanging in rope fingers take sunlight:
We drowse on a green bed in the valley of the third thing.

Here, among the thirty thousand days of a long life,
a single day stands still: The sun shines, it is raining;
we sleep, we make love, we plant a tree, we walk up and down
eating lunch: The day waits at the center when I reached out
to touch the face in the mirror, and never
touched glass, touched neither cheekbone nor eyelid,
touched galaxies instead and the void they hung on.
The one day extended from that moment, unrolling
continuous as the broad moon on water, or as motions of rain
that journey a million times through air to water.

Years later when I fell down drunk in Albany,
at the bus depot, among strangers, in rage and confusion,
when police behaved rudely to me, when I was nothing,
the day regarded me from its green distance
with pity — bewildered, yet steadfast as bread or apples.
When I woke again in the yellow Albany morning,
the day resided with me still. The wrist's knuckle
celebrates only the deject passion of self-regard;
cigarette smoke builds a house of daydream or idleness
to mimic clapboard and granite of the house we live in.

The one day speaks of July afternoons, of February
when snow builds shingle in spruce, when the high sugarmaple
regards the abandoned barn tilted inward, moving
in storm like Pilgrims crossing the Atlantic under sail.
The one day recalls us to hills and meadows, to moss,
roses, dirt, apples, and the breathing of timothy —
away from the yellow chair, from blue smoke and daydream.
Leave behind appointments listed on the printout!
Leave behind manila envelopes! Leave dark suits behind,
boarding passes, and soufflés at the chancellor's house!

The great rock at the side of the road reminds us.
Long ago we slipped, rodents among ferns like redwoods;
elongating our claws we climbed the baobab;
for millennia we hung by one hand eating with the other
until we dropped to hide in lengthening grass;
by the waterhole we walked upright sniffing for cats;
we chased elephants into the bog with our brothers;
for ten thousand years we scudded beneath bushes: I leaned
from ladder into tree; you watered the Burgundy Lily.
When we die it is the cell's death in a hair-end.

At the close of one day, nearly overcome by shadow,
the breath makes permanent house: spirit never visible.
Because we never catch glimpse of it, unobserved
it animates the day, like wellwater
after harvesting under September sun; like my mother's
painful hand that rubbed my father's head all night
when he lay dying; like the color green. Nebuchadnezzar
and the grocer fish with the same pole:
Nebuchadnezzar listens to his chief of staff complaining;
the grocer's son has broken his arm in Texas.

I walk around a corner in the strange town and arrive
at the first street of my childhood — the house half-blue,
half-yellow, the black Pierce-Arrow beside it. The tomcat
plays with his mother, sucking and teasing; he cuffs
his mother's jaw. The tomcat limps home in the bloody
morning, ear torn. The tomcat sleeps all day
in a portion of sun, fur tatty over old scars, pulls
himself to the saucer of milk, and snores going back
to sleep, knowing himself the same. The kitten leaps
in the air, her paws spread like a squirrel's.

The one day stands unmoving in sun and shadow:
like the tuft of grass left behind in the pasture
when the Holstein heard the farmer call her for milking
and remembered fresh millet; like Tunisian aqueducts
and butcherblock counters; like Blackwater Pond
with its dirt road; like the committee's styrofoam cup
that lives so briefly to contain coffee and its whitener
for ten minutes between the cellophaned stack
and the trash compactor; like the granite boulder
that the glacier deposited by the orchard's creek.

We visit our friends in their house at the town's edge.
My best friend is fifty now, his wife ten years younger.
They have a stout, strong baby named for a president
who stands in his highchair adorned with oatmeal
and waves his fists over his head like a boxer,
making bird-noises and laughing. As we watch
the vigorous father and mother laughing with their son,
we know that they undertake with energy
to enter the final determination of their lives;
in muscular bodies they walk to their deaths together.

Now as sun elicits seed planted after the full
moon's last frost in the springtime; or as crops ripen
south to north in August, slowly, as corn turns
green to gold; or as leaves redden in the northcountry,
gradually at first, a few branches, then whole trees led
by carmine swampmaples, hillsides brilliant overnight,
and then leaves falling, fading in November rain —
so their deaths enter upon them, while their brash
baby makes bird-noises standing in his highchair,
the invisible death hatching inside him also.

We return to inhabit this old house over Bone's orchard
that we will abandon in death only, our bodies slow
to assemble each morning as we gaze north at our trees.
We congregate, we grow to diminish again, we drowse.
I remember the dead fox warm on the barn floor,
inexplicably dead, and how my grandmother tenderly
lifted the body on her pitchfork, strands of hay
under the delicate corpse of the young red fox,
to the burying place by the willow at the garden's edge
where we left the barncat's kittens killed in the road.

When my body shook again with the body's passion,
it was possible only because I expected nothing.
The storm's rake that uprooted rockmaples granted
shape to the hill. Of course I must visit again
the burnt car and the sodality of white houses
where a wretched child stands carrying toys and staring
under the sun that will not let her sleep.
I will never read again the inscription, false with clarity,
that once I lived by; neither will I deny
the unreadable book printed from these abandonments.

There is also the day of general anaesthesia, when one
pushes the other's stretcher into the elevator
that descends to the operating room in the dark of dawn.
When the surgeon telephones midmorning he reports
cancer. As you return from Recovery I sit by your bed
to tell you. No one else may tell you.
For a week, as the pathologist studies dyed tissue,
we hold each other, we weep, we repeat reasonable
words of reassurance; but the mind projects
reel after reel of horror, pity, and self-pity.

The bed is a world of pain and the repeated deaths
of preparation for death. The awake nightmare
comforts itself by painting the mourner's portrait:
As I imagine myself on grief's rack at graveside
I picture and pity myself. When pathology supplies
the jargon of reassurance, I have buried your body
a thousand times. Gradually we recover pulse
to return to the bed's world and the third thing:
Still the stretcher forever enters the elevator going
down, and the telephone lacerates silence.

Now the lost friend or the repudiated self
sinks into wood of the table, throat heaving with veins,
hands trembling to hold the beer for waking up with,
tumbler of whiskey to steady his hands until lunch.
He is fat now, transparent hanging flesh, and he sighs
for lost love and betrayed day: — for what he wanted.
Or he walks the criminal's yard in the penitentiary
at Clinton, cursing and mumbling, seeing no one,
tracks on his arm scabbed over — that one shaking there,
gray-faced, who once was eager in pursuit of honor:

He walks delicately, impeccably, trembling in outrage,
among criminals in New York, like a sick fox
seeking the hay floor. When my sister drowns
my lungs fill also: We are one cell perpetually
dying and being born, led by a single day that presides
over our passage through the thirty thousand days
from highchair past work and love to suffering death.
We plant; we store the seedcorn. Our sons and daughters
topdress old trees. Two chimneys require:
Work, love, build a house, and die. But build a house.

Now pews fill for a Baptism; now white doors open
on a weekday for a funeral: — We file past the raised
lid of a coffin, confirming, and bury our neighbor
in the churchyard's village where flags fray over graves
of the 24th New Hampshire Volunteers under hemlocks
as dark as shutters. If once a lay preacher stole
collection money; if a deacon hanged himself in his barn,
each December Advent circles to return, and Advent's
child parches each spring on the hill shaped like a skull.
On the first Sunday of every month we assemble

molecules of Jesus from their diaspora and drive
downward to the dead of Zion's parish. As we pray
for the unborn they look backward upon us. The day
solves itself in love and work because the hands
of the hospice worker and her voice provide connection.
When the rain drives on the poppies they hold bright
petals to the rain. From pew to pew we construct together
geographies of a day: Once in Beijing at Easter,
in the eight-sided wooden church, the choir's Chinese
voices ascended in hymn, and up from the grave He arose.

When I was ninety I spent my days beside the window,
looking at birds from my wheelchair; sometimes I sketched.
To go to the White House for the President's Medal,
I needed help, and the Secret Service was helpful.
I omitted my diuretic that morning; that day I fasted.
A limousine took me to the air base where I was hoisted
into Air Force One for the brief flight to Andrews.
I remember little of the day, although with old friends
gathered for the ceremony I chatted about the past.
I felt no pain except when I stood for the medal.

This morning we watch tall poppies light up
in a field of grass. At the town dump, one styrofoam cup
endures eight hundred years. Under the barn,
fat and ancient grandfather spider sleeps
among old spoked wheels: Our breathing shakes his web:
It is always this time; the time that we live by
is this time. Together we walk in the high orchard
at noon; it is cool, although the sun poises upon us.
Among old trees the creek breathes slowly,
bordered by fern. The toad at our feet holds still.

We enter and explore this house, moving from room to room, surprised sometimes by décor, always remaining within the single structure. Or so I hope. One consciousness may contain everything that ever happened or might happen. Montaigne's *"form* of man's estate" may be rendered *template*.

The poem began in the fall of 1971. Beginning to emerge from a bad patch of middle-life, I was briefly subject to long and frequent attacks of language. I wrote as rapidly as I could, page after page, loose free verse characterized by abundance and strangeness rather than by anything else, certainly not by art nor the discipline of imagination. The meteor shower continued for several weeks. If I drove to the supermarket I carried a notebook; I might stop three times in a ten-minute journey to take dictation. It *seemed* like dictation, and although sometimes I knew from what part of my life certain lines started, at other times everything was strange — as if I received signals from other lives.

When it stopped I looked at what I had — and I did not know what it was. Much frightened me. Every now and then, over the next few years, lines would occur that announced themselves as part of the body of this work, which I began to call *Building the House of Dying*. I accumulated another dozen passages to add to the sixty or seventy pages that had come in the first onslaught. Sometimes in old notebooks I found lines written in the fifties and sixties that reminded me of *Building;* I copied them out; there are lines here that go back thirty years.

From time to time I looked at the disordered heap, to see what I could make of it. Many times I put it away in discouragement and

fear. Finally in 1979 or 1980 I was able to work. I separated it orig-
inally into twenty-five or thirty units of several pages each. I worked
for a year or two, showing it to no one. When I didn't know what to
do next, I read it aloud to my wife, Jane Kenyon — and then put it
away for a year. During that year a friend in a letter suggested that I
might be a poet to write a sequence, like Lowell's *Notebooks* or Berry-
man's 77 *Dream Songs*. Thinking about his suggestion I arrived at my
form: I would shape this material into ten-line bricks which could
build the house and remain whole.

When I worked again, maybe 1981, the poem began to fall into
three parts. I understood that a variety of voices spoke. One resembled
my own; others were alternates. It's a commonplace of psychiatry that
it may be useful, thinking about a dream, to consider that all of its
characters are versions of the dreamer. Picasso said that every human
being is a colony. Notions of human multiplicity, derived from ex-
perience, make the structure of this poem; but in the usual Heraclitan
truth of contradiction, the multiple is also singular.

Here two characters speak and each quotes others. When the woman
sculptor speaks, her words are in italics. The male "I," who will be
taken as the author, and who in the third section grows apples with
his wife, speaks in a roman typeface. But many roman lines belong to
a general consciousness that narrates. The two characters appear in
the first and third sections of this poem. In the middle part, "Four
Classic Texts," certain themes from the rest of the poem take over to
enact themselves in dreamlike monstrosity.

But I talk too much. As with many things I have written, I began not knowing what I was doing; I end seventeen years later, knowing a *lot* about what I have done . . . but if I am lucky I do not know everything; the best part is what you *never* know. Everything here is intended, by not being crossed out. Nothing was meant when I wrote it down; afterwards I concentrated to decide whether to keep what I wrote down. This form of composition grows a poem cell by cell like coral. If I succeed, the surface of the poem should look smooth but, like the great console radios of my youth, when you look behind this façade you see a maze of tubes and wires to connect everything with everything else. If I succeed, this poem is impulse validated by attention.

There are many borrowings and allusions. I have used Virgil, Amos and Isaiah, the words of a German soldier in the Great War, and stories from Livy and the *Boston Globe*. When I have borrowed I have altered. Some lines that resemble allusion or reference are fiction; there is considerable fiction here.

In *The Happy Man* I named people who have helped me; they continue. I neglected to name Robert Mazzocco and Wendell Berry. Alistair Elliot, Robert McDowell, and Peter Davison helped me with this poem.

THE ONE DAY

was typeset by Heritage Printers in Linotype Fairfield, a face drawn by Rudolph Ruzicka. The book was designed by Anne Chalmers and was printed and bound by The Book Press, Brattleboro, Vermont.